MW01139226

APP

I Can Make a Difference

Helping Family and Friends

Vic Parker

Heinemann Library
Chicago, Illinois

www.capstonepub.com
Visit our website to find out more information about Heinemann-Raintree books.

To order:
☎ Phone 888-454-2279
▱ Visit www.capstonepub.com
   to browse our catalog and order online.

© 2012 Heinemann Library
an imprint of Capstone Global Library, LLC
Chicago, Illinois

All rights reserved. No part of this publication may be reproduced or transmitted in any form or by any means, electronic or mechanical, including photocopying, recording, taping, or any information storage and retrieval system, without permission in writing from the publisher.

Edited by Daniel Nunn, Rebecca Rissman, and Sian Smith
Designed by Steve Mead
Picture research by Ruth Blair
Production by Eirian Griffiths
Originated by Capstone Global Library Ltd
Printed and bound in China by South China Printing Company Ltd

15 14 13 12 11
10 9 8 7 6 5 4 3 2 1

Library of Congress Cataloging-in-Publication Data
Parker, Victoria.
  Helping family and friends / Victoria Parker.—1st ed.
    p. cm.—(I can make a difference)
  Includes bibliographical references and index.
  ISBN 978-1-4329-5944-9 (hb)
  ISBN 978-1-4329-5949-4 (pb)
  1. Voluntarism. I. Title.
  HN49.V64P37 2012
  302'.14—dc22   2011015687

Acknowledgments
We would like to thank the following for permission to reproduce photographs: Corbis pp. 7 (© Hill Street Studios/Blend Images), 8 (© Roy McMahon), 10 (© Simon D. Warren), 12 (© moodboard), 15, 17 (© Ocean), 16 (© David P. Hall), 20 (© Image Source), 24 (© Andersen Ross/Blend Images), 27 (© Simon Jarratt), 29 (© JLP/Jose L. Pelaez); Getty Images p. 26 (Tim Platt/Iconica); Photolibrary pp. 18 (Jon Feingersh Photography/Superstock), 21 (SW Productions), 23 (Radius Images); Science Photo Library pp. 13 (DEV CARR, CULTURA), 22 (BSIP, GIRAL); Shutterstock pp. 4 (© wavebreakmedia ltd), 6 (© Gorilla), 9 (© Marcel Mooij), 11 (© Monkey Business Images), 14 (© Aletia), 19 (© sonya etchison), 25 (© wavebreakmedia ltd).

Cover photograph of a child helping in the kitchen reproduced with permission of Shutterstock (© Monkey Business Images).

Every effort has been made to contact copyright holders of any material reproduced in this book. Any omissions will be rectified in subsequent printings if notice is given to the publisher.

Disclaimer
All the Internet addresses (URLs) given in this book were valid at the time of going to press. However, due to the dynamic nature of the Internet, some addresses may have changed, or sites may have changed or ceased to exist since publication. While the author and Publishers regret any inconvenience this may cause readers, no responsibility for any such changes can be accepted by either the author or the Publishers.

Contents

Some words are shown in bold, **like this**. You can find out what they mean by looking in the glossary.

Why Help?

Volunteering means spending your time and energy being helpful. Many people, animals, and places need all sorts of help. By helping, we can make the world a better, happier place.

Anyone can volunteer to help, young or old.

Knowing that you have been helpful can make you feel really good.

Volunteering can also give you the chance to:

- try new things

- learn useful skills

- make friends

- keep active

- have fun!

 Before you help anyone, always get permission from a parent or guardian.

How Can I Help My Family and Friends?

There are lots of ways you can help your family and friends. Help might be something small, like watering a houseplant, or something bigger, like watering the whole yard.

If you would like to help, but don't know how to do something, just ask.

You can **volunteer** to do one-time jobs, for example, sticking stamps onto envelopes. Or you can volunteer to help with things that need doing regularly, such as unpacking the groceries.

Children are better at doing some things than grown-ups, such as reaching low places.

Helping Around the House

Lots of jobs need doing regularly around your house, such as picking up and cleaning. If one person has to do all these jobs, he or she might get tired and bored. If you **volunteer** to help, the jobs will be finished faster.

Volunteering to pick up and clean your bedroom is a great way to help.

Think about when your help is and isn't needed.

Maybe you could volunteer to do jobs at someone else's house, too. Do you have a friend or family member who is too busy to do jobs in their house, or who finds some of them difficult?

Feeding Family and Friends

Helping at mealtimes is another great way to **volunteer**. There may be things you can help with, such as tossing salad or mashing potatoes. Don't forget to wash your hands first!

You could volunteer to wash vegetables or fruit.

You could volunteer to set the table before a meal and clear away dishes afterward. There's always the dish washing and drying to help with, too.

You can volunteer to help at mealtimes whether you're at your own house or a friend's.

 Don't clean or clear away sharp knives.
Ask an adult to help with these.

Recycling Garbage

It is helpful to keep our planet healthy by turning garbage into new, useful things, rather than just throwing it away. You can help do this by **volunteering** to collect your family's used paper, cardboard, and plastic for **recycling**.

You could make it your job to rinse out your family's used plastic containers for recycling.

Sorting things into recycling bins can be satisfying and fun.

Don't forget to help put out your recycling for collection, or to help take it to your local recycling center. You might be able to help a friend or family member with this, too.

 Be very careful when handling things made from glass.

Helping With Little Ones

Do you know anyone who has a baby? They will be really busy and very glad if you offer to help. For instance, you could **volunteer** to pick up things they need, such as wipes, diapers, and bottles.

Helping someone look after a baby is very thoughtful.

If you know someone with a **toddler**, you could volunteer to play with the child for a while so that they can have a break.

Make sure you do one of the toddler's favorite things, rather than one of yours!

Helping Outside

If you like being outdoors, there are lots of ways you can **volunteer** to help outside. Maybe you could help a family member or friend wash their car.

Washing a car can be great fun.

Make sure you wear the right clothes when helping outdoors.

You can also help family or friends by helping pick up outside. Perhaps you could put toys away, pick up litter, or sweep up leaves.

Looking After Family Pets

Do you love animals? If your family has a pet, you could **volunteer** to feed it regularly. Make sure you use the right sort of food and the right amount, or you might make the animal sick.

Sometimes volunteering can be unhelpful, like if you feed fish too much or too often.

You could volunteer to help somebody by keeping them company on a dog walk.

There are plenty of other ways you can care for a pet, such as brushing a dog or cleaning out a hamster's cage. If you do not have a pet, volunteer to help with a friend's pet.

Visiting People

You may have a family member or a friend who cannot get out much. It would cheer them up a lot if you **volunteered** to visit them regularly.

Always ask your parent or guardian to take you on a visit.

You could take the person a card, picture, or cake you have made for them. They may also like you to read to them, especially if you have written the story yourself.

A **homemade** gift will really cheer someone up.

Donating

Do you have any toys, games, or clothes that you no longer need? You can help friends or family members by offering these things to them instead. This is called **donating**.

Make sure the things you give away are still in good condition.

You could make a voucher promising to help hang out the washing.

You can give your time, as well as **belongings**, to family and friends, too. For presents, you can make "promise" **vouchers** they can use when they like, such as a voucher promising to help with making the bed.

Thinking Small

Often, the smallest things can be the most helpful. For example, you could **volunteer** to carry your own backpack, open a door for someone, or pick up something they have dropped.

When you help people in small ways, it can make a big difference to them.

You can help other people by understanding what they need.

Sometimes, it is helpful to volunteer *not* to do things, too. For example, if your parent has a headache, you could volunteer *not* to play noisy games or watch television loudly, but do something quiet instead.

Thinking Big

You may have a family member or friend who needs big help, such as money for special medical equipment. If so, you will have to ask lots of people to help you.

You could ask your friends at school if they want to **volunteer** with you.

Great ways for a group to raise money include holding a sale of **donated** things or of baked goods you have made. You could all do a **sponsored** event, where people promise to give you money for completing a challenge, such as not talking for a long time.

These people are doing a sponsored walk.

Volunteer Checklist

To be a good **volunteer**, you need to:

- be interested and have lots of energy

- think about other people

- work out what you can do to help

- share and take turns, if you are in a team

- be friendly

- keep your promises.

Most importantly, *always* check with your parent or guardian before you volunteer to help outside your home. Then they can make sure that you will be safe. They may even want to help!

Working with other people you know well can be a safe way to volunteer.

Glossary

belongings things that you own

donate to give away something that is of use to someone else

homemade something you have made yourself instead of buying it from a store

recycling breaking down materials and using them again to make new things

sponsor to pay money to someone for completing a challenge. The money is then used to help someone or something.

toddler very young child who has just learned to walk

volunteer offer to do something. Someone who offers to do something is called a volunteer.

voucher piece of paper that can be used by someone to get something in return. The writing on a voucher explains what you can get with it.

Find Out More

Books

Olien, Rebecca. *75 Ways to Make a Difference for People, Animals and the Environment (Kids Care!)* Danbury, Conn.: Ideals Publishing Corporation, 2007.

Parr, Todd. *The Family Book*. New York: Little, Brown, 2010.

Schuette, Sarah. *Families (People)*. Mankato, Minn.: Capstone, 2009.

Websites

kidshealth.org/kid/feeling/thought/volunteering.html
Find out about how families can volunteer.

pbskids.org/itsmylife/emotions/volunteering
This website will help you think about how you could begin volunteering.

www.volunteermatch.org
This website has the details of thousands of organizations that need volunteers.

Index